How To Release
the Power of God

D1636948

by
John Osteen

Contents

Chapter 1

The Purpose of Pentecost

The eternal God, who cannot lie, has made the human race a promise. It is found in the Book of Joel. *And it shall come to pass afterward that I will pour out my spirit upon all flesh* (2:28). This promise is being fulfilled today!

Ministers and members of all the historic denominations are receiving the baptism in the Holy Ghost as on the Day of Pentecost (see Acts 2). They are speaking in other tongues, prophesying, praying for the sick, casting out devils, and seeing miracles. The mighty gifts of the Spirit spoken of in 1 Corinthians 12 are being restored to the Body of Christ.

This movement of God's Spirit has caught the attention of the secular press. National magazines and newspapers are reporting this ever-increasing movement within the denominational world.

Why is God baptizing people in the Holy Ghost? What is the purpose of this wonderful experience? Does it meet any need? Does it help us fulfill our biblical destiny? What is the purpose of Pentecost?

Is the baptism in the Holy Ghost given just to

make a person feel good or shout and praise the Lord? Is the baptism in the Holy Ghost given to help believers start a new denomination and proselyte from all the existing ones? Is it given just to make us speak in tongues?

The answer to all of these questions is no. The baptism in the Holy Ghost will make you feel good and shout and praise the Lord. You will speak in tongues as they did in Acts, chapters 2, 10, and 20. But we dare not miss the *real* purpose of this experience.

In 1958, as a Southern Baptist minister, I set my heart to seek the Lord. I did so because I was burdened to do something for Him. Time was flying and men were dying. It seemed I had done so little for Jesus since being saved in 1939. As I sought the Lord and read His Word, I began to see that humanity was in the grip of the satanic powers of hell. They were being held captive and they were blinded. I saw Satan going forth as a roaring lion to kill, steal, and destroy. I saw that Jesus came as the mighty conqueror to destroy the works of the devil. He said, ''All power is given to Me in Heaven and earth. Ye shall receive power after the Holy Ghost has come upon you.'' I needed this power. When I fasted and prayed before the Lord I was burdened to win the lost and bring deliverance to suffering humanity. I *needed* power! I *wanted* power!

When I received the baptism in the Holy Ghost, I spoke in other tongues and have continued to do so almost every day since that wonderful time. Far be it from me to play down or belittle speaking in tongues. I say, with the Apostle Paul, *I would that ye all spake in tongues* (1 Corinthians 14:5) and *Forbid not to speak with tongues* (1 Corinthians 14:39). My desire is to be like him when he said, *I thank my God, I speak with tongues more than ye all* (1 Corinthians 14:18). What a thrill for the blessed Spirit of God to move upon us, enabling us to pray in other languages or give a message in tongues for the edification of the Church! How poor spiritually is the person who has never spoken in tongues!

Power to reach the lost

The Lord Jesus did not baptize me in the Holy Ghost just so I could speak in tongues but that I might have power to reach a lost world. He let me speak in tongues so I would know that I had received the baptism in the Holy Ghost. But the purpose of this experience was to give me **power**.

In the Book of Joel, the Lord tells us the purpose of this great outpouring of the Spirit. He says, *Proclaim ye this among the Gentiles* [heathen]. *Let the heathen be wakened. Put ye in the sickle, for the harvest is ripe. Multitudes, multitudes in the valley of decision* (Joel 3:9,12-14).

The masses of common, neglected, poverty-stricken people throughout the entire world are stirring. They want help. Their hands are outstretched and their hearts are open. The harvest is ripe! The purpose of this mighty outpouring of the Holy Ghost is to empower the Church to take the Gospel of Jesus Christ to this needy world. These waiting multitudes will believe and receive Christ when they see Him perform miracles as He did in the Bible!

Ordinary methods will not work. Modern denominationalism, which has been robbed of the supernatural, has no appeal to these distraught, demon-oppressed captives. Jesus is baptizing people in the Holy Ghost and fire that they may, through signs, miracles, and wonders, convince these awakened multitudes that Jesus is alive from the dead and will save unto the uttermost those who come to God by Him.

Stay on the right track

Satan would like to sidetrack this great move of God. In some instances he has. Many people who seek this experience are not concerned for a lost and needy world. Many who have received the Baptism seem to have forgotten about the purpose of this enduement of power. If all you want to do is talk in tongues then you have distorted the whole meaning of this divine visitation.

Hundreds of potential soulwinners who could bring deliverance in the Name of Jesus are caught up in the thrill of some ''new'' revelation or some directive prophecy or some strange visitation and have no burden for the lost. Because they have missed the whole purpose of this power, they have gone astray into many beliefs and doctrines which are not biblical. They lose respect for the divinely appointed ministries Christ has given His Body. They become exalted, confused, defeated, and finally make shipwreck of their testimony.

Jesus said, *The Spirit of the Lord is upon me, because he hath anointed me to preach the gospel to the poor; he hath sent me to heal the brokenhearted, to preach deliverance to the captives, and recovering of sight to the blind, to set at liberty them that are bruised, to preach the acceptable year of the Lord* (Luke 4:18,19).

Jesus said, *Ye shall receive power, after that the Holy Ghost is come upon you: and ye shall be witnesses unto me both in Jerusalem, and in all Judaea, and in Samaria, and unto the uttermost part of the earth* (Acts 1:8).

Mark 16:15 says, *Go ye into all the world, and preach the gospel to **every creature** and these signs shall follow them that believe. . . .* God has not promised these signs to those who only want to go to their select group or just their denomination. He said, "*All* the world and *every* creature." This power is not just for a select group but for every creature. If you are burdened for this lost world and desire every creature to hear the Good News, then signs and miracles will attend your life to help you effectively meet their needs.

God has not given us His precious Holy Spirit to enjoy alone and forget the needs of the world. It is not His purpose for us to get together just to shout, jump, prophesy over each other, and feast upon some "new" revelation while the world rushes on toward hell. The Lord didn't command us to go deep, but *go out* to all the world!

There is so little time left. May God help us to channel this great outpouring of the Holy Ghost into its rightful purpose — taking the Gospel to every creature through mighty signs and wonders in the Name of Jesus.

Chapter 2

How To Release the Power of God

God's power is released in the behalf of some. Others seem to always fail to touch God, and benefit from His delivering power. Is it God's plan to only use a few? Can all expect God to use them?

Why do some experience miracles in their own lives, becoming channels for God's power to flow out to others to deliver them from fear, sickness, sin, and demon power, while others dedicate themselves sincerely to God, fast and pray, and go forth only to fail to see God's power released and demonstrated?

The Word of God is plain that God wants and expects to use all His children to help bring His loving compassion and power to every generation. The very fact that you have a desire to be used and are now reading these words in hope of finding the secret is evidence that God has put it in your heart and destined to make you a channel of His delivering power.

The Bible says, *These signs shall follow them that believe; In my name shall they cast out devils; they shall speak with new tongues; They shall take up serpents; and if they drink any deadly thing it shall not hurt them;*

they shall lay hands on the sick, and they shall recover (Mark 16:17,18).

The Lord says, *But the manifestation of the Spirit is given to every man. The Spirit of God,* [divides] *to every man severally as he will* (1 Corinthians 12:7,11).

Jesus said to us all, *Verily, verily, I say unto you, He that believeth on me, the works that I do shall he do also; and greater works than these shall he do; because I go unto my Father. And whatsoever ye shall ask in my name, that will I do that the Father may be glorified in the Son. If ye shall ask any thing in my name, I will do it* (John 14:12-14).

But how can we get these things to come to pass?

Doing what Jesus did

When Peter saw Jesus walking on the water, he asked Jesus to let him walk on the water also. Jesus did not rebuke him and tell him to stay in the boat. Jesus was thrilled that Peter wanted to do what he saw his Master do. Jesus said to Peter, "Come!" And Peter did the same supernatural thing that Jesus did.

You, like Peter, have seen Jesus doing the supernatural. You have followed Him in the Bible, and watched Him heal the sick, deliver the oppressed, and set the captives free. This thrilled you and made you want to do what Jesus did. Jesus does not rebuke you in displeasure for this desire. He gave it to you. He wants you to launch out and do what He did. He is saying, "Come out of your little denominationalized boat, which has kept you from these things, and walk with Me in the supernatural realm that I have planned for you."

You are determined to obey His voice. You are

willing to pay any price. You want to know how to get the power of God released and how you can help humanity.

The importance of the Word of God

The secret of getting God on the scene and working in behalf of needy humanity has to do with His divine Word given forth in the power of the Holy Ghost. They preached the Gospel with the power the Holy Ghost sent down from Heaven.

Hear what God says about His eternal Word: *So shall my word be that goeth forth out of my mouth: it shall not return unto me void, but it shall accomplish that which I please, and it shall prosper in the thing whereto I sent it* (Isaiah 55:11).

The angel said to Mary, "No Word of God shall be void of power" (see Luke 1:37,38).

Hebrews 4:12 says, *The Word of God is quick, and powerful, and sharper than any two-edged sword, piercing even to the dividing asunder of soul and spirit, and of the joints and marrow, and is a discerner of the thoughts and intents of the heart.*

Joshua said, *There failed not aught of any good thing which the Lord had spoken . . . all came to pass* (Joshua 21:45).

Jesus said, *Heaven and earth shall pass away, but my words shall not pass away* (Matthew 24:35).

The Bible says that God watches over His Word to perform it (see Jeremiah 1:12).

In the beginning was the Word, and the Word was with God, and the Word was God (John 1:1).

God spoke the words of the Bible. He is behind every word and in every word. And God watches over

13

every promise to make it good.

Jesus said, *If thou canst believe, all things are possible to him that believeth* (Mark 9:23). The Lord declares, *Without faith it is impossible to please him* (Hebrews 22:6).

If we can only get faith into our hearts and into the hearts of those who need help, then God will work in a miraculous way.

Where does faith come from?

But where does faith come from? How can we get it? The Bible says, *Faith cometh by hearing and hearing by the Word of God* (Romans 10:17).

If you don't have faith, you can get faith to come to you and live in your heart. If your needy friends don't have faith, you can get faith to come into their lives also. What makes faith arise from the throne of God and walk, run, or fly into our lives and produce the mighty works of God?

Faith comes by hearing the Word of God!

You cannot see God work without faith, for without faith it is impossible to please Him. You cannot have Bible faith without the Word of God.

The secret is to give people the Word of God. There can be no salvation, no healing, no miracles apart from Bible faith and this only comes from hearing, receiving, and acting on the promises in the Word of God.

Give people the Word

Once, while in a crusade in one of the communist states of India, I faced about a thousand people who had come to hear what was being said. They were

Hindus, Moslems, communists, and other non-believers. As I looked into their faces and saw the fear, sadness, turmoil, suffering, and hopelessness, my heart cried out to help them. There were so many sick, blind, deaf, crippled, and deformed among them. How could I help them? What could I do?

I did just exactly what I am telling you in these pages. I knew that they had to have faith. The only way faith could be produced was to give them the Word of God. I gave them the promises of God. I preached the Gospel. And as I explained the cross, the blood of Jesus, His burial and resurrection, faith began to rise in their hearts. Suddenly faith went to work. They began to receive Jesus into their hearts and eternal life was imparted to them. Then the Lord answered the cry of their faith in the matter of healing and deliverance.

The deaf, crippled, blind, deformed, and diseased came to tell of God's great mercy in healing and delivering them. It was no wonder the crowds grew by the thousands each night. Estimates of 15 to 20 thousand people gathered in a single service before the end of the campaign.

How could all of this happen? It happened because I had learned what I am passing on to you in the hope that you will also benefit from these testimonies.

I knew *without* faith, God would not be pleased to work.

I knew that *with* faith all things were possible.

I knew that the only way to produce faith in their hearts was by the Word of God for faith comes by hearing the Word of God.

I simply gave them the Gospel. And as the Word

of God went forth, faith was produced and they found God present in mighty power to save and deliver, because they believed and acted on His promises.

Perhaps you have a friend, a relative, or some other person who needs the miracle touch of God. You have talked with them, pleaded with them, but still they do not get saved or healed. You have even prayed long hours with fasting but nothing happens. Nothing will ever happen without faith coming into their hearts, and faith only comes by hearing the Word of God!

The Word will produce faith

Simply obey this spiritual law. To get God to work, faith must be in the heart. To get faith into the heart, we must present the Word of God, and let it produce faith in a person's heart. Then, when faith arises in the heart and the promises are received and acted upon, God moves to back up His Word and miracles take place.

Go give them the promises. Go back and give them some more promises. Return and share again the things God has done for them on the cross with the sacrifice of Jesus. Faith will come. It started the first day you gave the Word. Faith cometh. Don't be discouraged. Keep giving the Word of God and you will see God work in answer to the cry of that faith which is produced by believing the promises of God.

The only thing God has promised to confirm is His Word! *The Lord* [was] *working with them, and confirming the word with signs following* (Mark 16:20).

God works only in relation to His Word. When

16

He wanted to redeem mankind, He sent the Word and the Word became flesh in Jesus.

If we have none of the Word of God; if we leave it out or do not know it, and are too indifferent to study it, we cannot expect results. We may talk, reason, weep, and fast and pray, but unless we give out the Word of God, faith cannot come and without faith, nothing will be accomplished.

But you can be sure of this. *He that goeth forth and weepeth, bearing precious seed* [the Word of God], *shall doubtless come again with rejoicing, bringing his sheaves with him* (Psalm 126:6).

It takes individual faith

A person must have individual faith in his own heart for his own deliverance!

Jesus said to the blind man, *Go thy way; thy faith hath made thee whole* (Mark 10:52). To the woman who was healed of the issue of blood, He said, *Daughter, thy faith hath made thee whole* (Mark 5:34). He said to the two blind men, *According to your faith be it unto you* (Matthew 9:29), and they were healed.

If you need help, then you must have faith. If your friend or relative needs help, then they must have their own faith. For faith to be produced in my heart, your heart, or anyone's heart, the Word of God must be given to produce it.

While on a crusade in the Philippine Islands, I saw this demonstrated. About 5,000 people gathered for the first service. We broadcast the services live over two radio stations and hundreds of thousands of people in that section of the world were able to hear the Gospel. Testimonies of salvation and healing were given daily over the air. As a result, many came from afar to be saved and healed.

One day, a tall man in his late fifties came to me at my hotel. He was very plain in his dress. He said that he had come a long way to talk with me. I remember how sick he was. He told me about how he had suffered for such a long time. I asked him how long he could stay, purposing to invite him to the service that afternoon. Then he said a startling thing. "If you will heal me now, I will go on back home."

Never in my life have I seen a more disappointed man when I told him I could not heal him. He looked so whipped and defeated — as though he had lost his last chance in life. He asked about the many miracles he had heard about over the radio. I explained that the only way I could heal him was to give him the Gospel, and the promises of God, and lead him to believe for himself.

Well, he promised to stay. That afternoon he stood out in the open and listened to the Word of God. Afterwards I did not see him and wondered if he had gotten any help. But in the very next service, as we were having testimonies after the message, I saw him in the line to testify. He was grinning from ear to ear! The joy of the Lord was on his face. He came to the microphone and told how God had saved him and healed him of his sickness!

You see, we have to follow God's spiritual law — give the Word of God and let it produce faith. Faith receives and acts on the promises and God goes to work, fulfilling and confirming His Word.

Preach the Word

In Luke, chapter 4, Jesus opens the Bible and gives them a message. When He finishes, He says, "Today is this Scripture fulfilled." In other words, "Today this promise is good. Now is the time God will stand behind His promises. Expect God to do it now."

Notice what Jesus did. He first preached and taught the Word of God, and then He healed the sick.

In Mark, chapter 2, Jesus performed a mighty miracle. But notice first, "He preached the Word." The Bible says Jesus went about preaching and teaching and then healing all manner of sickness and all manner of diseases among the people (see Matthew 4:23).

Jesus honored the Word and preached the Word and so must we.

I went through a real learning experience while trying to win my Daddy to the Lord Jesus. I prayed for him. I cried out for God to save him. I talked with him. I reasoned with him, but all to no avail. He just couldn't believe. Faith was just not there to cry out to God for salvation.

How could that be? Faith does not come by begging, talking, reasoning, praying, or even weeping. Faith comes by hearing the Word of God. So I decided to do it God's way.

My family left me alone with Daddy in my sister's home in Dallas, Texas. They all went to other parts of the house to pray as I dealt with him.

What did I do? I gave him the Word of God. As I told him about Jesus, I read the Bible, explaining the Gospel and showing him the promises of God. I continued to do this and something began to happen.

Faith began to come! Now he had something and Someone to believe! Soon he gave his life to Jesus, accepting Him as his personal Savior! He is in Heaven today, simply because he heard the Word of God. The Word produced faith, and faith touched God for the miracle of salvation!

Jesus said in Mark 16:15, *Go ye into all the world, and preach the gospel to every creature . . . and these signs shall follow.* Go forth and preach, teach, tell, and share the Gospel in the power of the Holy Ghost. It will produce faith, and faith will move God to act and meet the needs of people in spirit, mind, and body.

Chapter 3

The Seed Is the Word

Our desire is to show you how to get the Word of God to work. How can you get it to produce results? You know the promises. You accept the Bible as true. Your desire is to get the same results in this generation as those in the Book of Acts. After all, *Jesus Christ the same yesterday, and to-day, and for ever* (Hebrews 13:8).

To be full of faith, you must be full of His Word. To be full of God, you must be full of His Word. To believe God is to believe His Word.

Jesus said, *A sower went out to sow his seed . . . The seed is the word of God* (Luke 8:5,11). Here God calls His Word SEED.

I suggest that you stop now and read from the Bible the complete parable of the sower found in the Gospel of Luke, chapter 8.

God shows us many pictures describing His Word. This is done so that we might understand how to release the mighty power in His Word. In order to show us how to get the Word to produce, He says, ''The seed is the Word of God.''

Just as all the beautiful seeds of the world could be laid on the shelves of our home and admired for their beauty, but never used to produce as they were intended, so God's Word could stay in our homes just as lifeless and fruitless.

We are willing to admire the Word of God, defend the Word of God, and treasure its presence in our homes. But what about its power? How can the power in these words of God be released? The seed is the Word of God. Just as you can release the power of seeds by obeying the laws of God in the natural world, you can release the power of the Word of God by obeying the same law in the spiritual realm.

Seeds carry life

A seed is a strange and awesome thing. Man can make something that looks exactly like it. It will be the same size, weight, and have the same component parts. It would be hard for an ordinary person to tell the difference between the real seed and the one made by man. But there is one vast difference.

The real seed has an indefinable quality about it. It has life! The other may look exactly like it, but it has no life! A real seed has life to reproduce itself many fold in a miraculous way.

There are millions of words in the world. They are in books, newspapers, and magazines. They are shaped like those in the Bible. They look just like those in the Bible. There is one difference. They have no real life.

The words in the Bible have an indefinable quality. They have God-breathed life in them! All Scripture is God-breathed. Jesus said, *The words that I* speak unto you, they are spirit, and they are life (John 6:63).

The Word of God . . . LIVETH and ABIDETH FOREVER (1 Peter 1:23, emphasis mine). *The Word of God is* [living]*, and powerful, and sharper than any two-edged sword* (Hebrews 4:12).

The Word of God is a living seed given to the sons of men. And God uses His Word as seed to produce a harvest!

You reap what you sow

The farmer uses seed to produce a crop. No farmer would expect to see a crop in his field without first sowing the seed. There can be no fruit without seed being planted. But so many of us expect God to work and produce the harvest of salvation, healing, miracles, and deliverance without first planting the seed which is the Word of God. To reap, there must first be the sowing. *Whatsoever a man soweth, that shall he also reap* (Galatians 6:7).

We have to determine what it is that we want from God. If we want apples, then plant apple seeds. If you want peaches, use peach seeds. The Scripture says, *Whatsoever a man soweth, that shall he also reap.* If you sow no seed, you get nothing. If you sow apple seeds, you get apples. It is as simple as that.

What is it you want from God? If you want healing, then sow healing seed! If you want a miracle, sow some miracle seeds! If you want deliverance from fear, habits, Satan's power, then get the appropriate seeds and sow them in your heart.

What is it that you want your friends or relatives to receive from God? Sow that kind of seed and you will surely reap, for *whatsoever a man soweth, that shall he also reap*.

Healing seed

To all of you who are now sick, or have someone who needs healing, I give these healing seeds. Say them out loud and listen to them. Plant them in the heart. They are alive, and will come forth with divine results. God's seeds for healing are these:

Surely He has borne our griefs — sickness, weakness and distress — and carried our sorrows and pain [of punishment]. Yet we ignorantly considered Him stricken, smitten and afflicted by God [as if with leprosy]. But He was wounded for our transgressions, He was bruised for our guilt and iniquities; the chastisement needful to obtain peace and well-being for us was upon Him, and with the stripes that wounded Him we are healed and made whole (Isaiah 53:4,5, Amplified).

I am the Lord that healeth thee (Exodus 15:26).

I will take sickness away from the midst of thee . . . the number of thy days I will fulfil (Exodus 23:25,26).

Who forgiveth all thine iniquities; who healeth all thy diseases (Psalm 103:3).

My God shall supply all your need according to his riches in glory by Christ Jesus (Philippians 4:19).

If ye shall ask any thing in my name, I will do it (John 14:14).

Attend to my words . . . They are life unto those that find them, and health to all their flesh (Proverbs 4:20,22).

These are the promises of God to YOU!

These are living seeds with divine potential. They will do you no good lying on the shelf, in the pages of the Bible. Seed must be planted in your heart. Put God's Word into your heart and nourish it daily with praise and thanksgiving. The harvest will surely come.

If you are seeking to help others, either as a minister or as a believer who is a member of a local church, then go sow these seeds in the heart of the one that you want to help. These words are "spirit and life," said Jesus. Like a seed, they will spring forth with a sure harvest.

A farmer may go weep over his field. He may pray much for his field and fast for it to bring forth fruit, but if he sows no seed in obedience to the natural laws of God, he will have no success! He may argue, "My God is a miracle-working God! He can do anything!" This is true, but God works in His own way. His thoughts are not our thoughts, and His ways are not our ways. We must find out God's ways of bringing about results. The farmer must plant the seed and let the power in the seed loose to do its work!

Are you weeping over a member of your family who is very much in need of healing? Are you fasting for results in your ministry? Are you wondering why God does not seem to hear you praying for healing in your own body?

Many of us have been in this same place. I know I have. But like the farmer, we will find all to no avail unless we plant the seed. Divine power comes only from divine seed, which is the Word of God.

The Bible is like a bag of seed. Each promise has the life of God breathed into it. Take the seed bag and start sowing in your own heart, and in the hearts of those you wish to help.

Salvation seeds

If it is salvation you want to produce, then sow these seeds:

For God so loved the world, that he gave his only begotten Son, that whosoever believeth in him should not perish, but have everlasting life (John 3:16).

Christ died for the ungodly (see Romans 5:16).

Christ died for sinners (see Romans 5:8).

All we like sheep have gone astray; we have turned every one to his own way; and the Lord hath laid on him [Jesus] *the iniquity of us all* (Isaiah 53:6).

Believe on the Lord Jesus Christ, and thou shalt be saved, and thy house (Acts 16:31).

As many as received him, to them gave he power to become the sons of God, even to them that believe on his name (John 1:12).

Whosoever shall call upon the name of the Lord shall be saved (Romans 10:13).

That if thou shalt confess with thy mouth the Lord Jesus, and shalt believe in thine heart that God hath raised him from the dead, thou shalt be saved. For with the heart man believeth unto righteousness; and with the mouth confession is made unto salvation (Romans 10:9,10).

Seeds for overcoming fear

If you want to overcome fear, then sow seeds like the following:

For he hath said, I will never leave thee, nor forsake thee. So that we may boldly say, The Lord is my helper, and I will not fear what man shall do unto me (Hebrews 13:6).

Fear thou not; for I am with thee: be not

dismayed; for I am thy God: I will strengthen thee; yea, I will help thee; yea I will uphold thee with the right hand of my righteousness (Isaiah 41:10).

Say with David, "Though I walk through the valley of the shadow of death, I will fear no evil. Though an host encamp against me, my heart shall not fear. God is my refuge and strength, a very present help in trouble. Therefore will we not fear though the earth be removed and the mountains thereof be carried into the midst of the sea."

Seeds for overcoming weakness and inability

If Satan has condemned you and oppressed you about your weakness and inability, then go to the "seed bag," which is the Word of God, and select the appropriate seed. For example, sow the following in your heart or in the hearts of those you wish to help:

Resist the devil, and he will flee from you (James 4:7).

The Son of God was manifested that he might destroy the works of the devil (1 John 3:8).

[He hath] *spoiled principalities and powers, he made a shew of them openly, triumphing over them* (Colossians 2:15).

Behold, I give unto you power to tread on serpents and scorpions, and over all the power of the enemy: and nothing shall by any means hurt you (Luke 10:19, see also Luke 9:1).

Say boldly as you plant these seeds in your heart, "I am a new creature in Christ Jesus. I have become a partaker of His divine nature. I have His blood, His righteousness, His peace, and His joy, and I can do all things through Christ who strengthens me. I am more

27

than a conqueror through Him that loved me. There is therefore now no condemnation to them that are in Christ Jesus, who walk not after the flesh, but after the Spirit. No weapon formed against me shall prosper, and every tongue that rises against me in judgment, I shall condemn. This is the heritage of the servants of the Lord and their righteousness is of me, saith the Lord.''

This seed will produce a harvest in your heart! Plant it! Nourish it! Confess it! And God will watch over His Word to perform it (see Jeremiah 1:12). No word of God shall be void of power (see Luke 1:37).

You will remember God said concerning the ones who had ''salvation seed'' sown in their hearts, [Ye were] *born again, not of corruptible seed, but of incorruptible, by the word of God, which liveth and abideth for ever* (1 Peter 1:23).

When a person is healed, it is through the incorruptible healing seed which is the Word of God. *He sent his word, and healed them* (Psalm 107:20).

When a person is delivered and helped in any way through faith, it is always through the incorruptible seed which is the Word of God.

Waiting for results

Now, normally, you have to sow and wait for results. But since this is miracle seed, God can command results immediately and results will come. This is so in salvation, when a person believes in and receives Jesus as Lord and Savior.

But do not lose heart if no immediate results are produced. Just like it takes time to produce a crop from planted seed, it often takes time to produce a crop from the seed of God's Word. In the natural, even though no results seem evident, these seeds are still at work on our behalf.

No farmer sows seed and then goes to dig it up every day or two to look at it. It would never grow that way. When a farmer sows in his field, he goes on his way and commits the seed to the earth and the laws of God. He knows the seed is working. Even though he can't see it working, he knows in his heart that it is working.

He proves it by his confession and actions! He talks about his crop as though it was a reality. All he has is seed in the ground! But to hear him talk, you would think that he already had the crop! He even plans how he will spend the money! He talks and acts like the harvest is a reality, because he knows that the seed is at work, according to the laws of God!

We need to do the same thing.

After the Word is sown, commit it to God and to His spiritual laws. *Keep* [the words] *in the midst of thine heart, for* [they are] *life unto those that find them, and health to all their flesh* (Proverbs 4:21,22). Talk like it is already a reality for God cannot lie. Make plans as though God would keep His promises. Your confession and actions will nourish and water the Word, and your results are sure to come.

Preparing the soil to receive the seed

Before a farmer can plant natural seed, he must properly prepare the soil. We, too, must be careful to prepare the soil of our heart before we sow the seed of the Word of God. In the parable of the sower in Luke 8, Jesus showed us three crop failures and one success.

The crop failures came not because of the failure of the Word of God, but because of the condition of the soil of the heart.

The first was a hard heart, which could not receive the Word, and Satan came and snatched it away *lest they should believe and be saved* (Luke 8:12). Satan knows that without the Word a person cannot be saved.

The second was a heart which seemed to be soft and receptive, but underneath was an unseen rock which prevented the seed from taking root. Hidden hardness and unconfessed sin — an unrepentant attitude or any form of insincerity — will keep the Word from producing. You may receive the Word with joy, but in time of temptation, you will become offended because of the Word.

The third was a heart which heard and received the Word, but it was filled with thorns which choked the Word. The heart that is full of the cares of this life, the deceitfulness of riches, and the lust of other things will surely choke the Word and it will not produce.

But the one which produced a harvest was *an honest and good heart* (vs. 15). A person who is honest with God — good enough to give God a chance, hears and understands the Word, takes the Word in sincerity and humility with dependence upon God and His power — is the person who will see God work in a miraculous way.

Remember: It's important to sow the seed of God's Word. *He that goeth forth and weepeth, bearing precious seed* [the Word of God]*, shall doubtless come again with rejoicing, bringing his sheaves with him* (Psalm 126:6).

He which soweth sparingly shall reap also sparingly; and he which soweth bountifully shall reap also bountifully (2 Corinthians 9:6). *For whatsoever a man soweth, that shall he also reap* (Galatians 6:7).

In the morning sow thy seed, and in the evening withhold not thine hand (Ecclesiastes 11:6).

Blessed are ye that sow beside all waters (Isaiah 32:20).

Chapter 4

Commanding Power

Satan has blinded the eyes of mankind as to the place God wants man to occupy. Satan wants us to think we are weak and unworthy. God wants us to see we can do all things through Christ who strengthens us (see Philippians 4:13).

No one would depreciate the place of prayer and the need of prayer. Jesus prayed all night and so should we. The Apostles said, *We will give ourselves continually to prayer, and to the ministry of the word* (Acts 6:4).

But we must rise up from prayer, believing we have been heard. We must go forth like Jesus who said at the grave of Lazarus, "Father, I thank Thee that Thou hast heard Me," and then commanded Lazarus to come forth from the grave!

Jesus made it plain that He has given us power in His Name over demons, sickness, and disease. He said to His disciples, [I give you] *power against unclean spirits, to cast them out, and to heal all manner of sickness and all manner of disease. As ye go, preach . . . heal the sick, cleanse the lepers, raise the dead,* cast out devils: *freely ye have received, freely give* (Matthew 10:1,7,8).

That's why Paul could say to the demon-possessed woman in Acts 16:18, *I command thee in the name of Jesus Christ to come out of her. And he came out the same hour.*

And to the lame man at the gate Peter said, *Silver and gold have I none; but such as I have give I thee: In the name of Jesus Christ of Nazareth rise up and walk* (Acts 3:6).

The Lord is saying in plain words, "I give *you* power. I give this power to YOU! Don't ask Me to heal, YOU heal the sick! Don't ask Me to cast out devils, YOU cast them out in my Name! Don't ask Me to deliver, YOU deliver the people through the power I have given you as My disciples!"

Understand who you are

I am convinced that this is where many of us fail. It's not a matter of being lifted up in false pride, but of understanding who we are through God's grace and mercy, and what He has promised to do through us because of the death, burial, and resurrection of Jesus Christ our Savior.

Who are we as Christians? We are new creatures in Christ Jesus, bone of His bone and flesh of His flesh! We have become partakers of His divine nature with His blood over us, His eternal life in us, and His Spirit empowering us. He has given us His joy, His righteousness, His peace, His Name, His life, and His power!

He said, *Verily, verily, I say unto you, He that believeth on me, the works that I do shall he do also;*

34

and greater works than these shall he do; because I go unto my Father (John 14:12).

If ye shall ask [or demand to be done] *any thing in my name, I will do it* (John 14:14).

God has invited us to enter into such a ministry. *Call unto me, and I will answer thee, and shew thee great and mighty things, which thou knowest not* (Jeremiah 33:3).

Realizing who we are and what God has promised we could do in the Name of Jesus, we should rise up and exercise commanding power. We are sons and daughters of God. He said that He has given us power through the Name of Jesus to command demons, sickness, trouble, and disease to leave, and it will come to pass!

My sister's healing

My sister was desperately ill a few years ago. She was confined to her bed continually with 24-hour nursing care. She had been sent home from the hospitals after they had done all they could for her. Her condition did not get better, but rather grew worse. She could not walk. She could not feed herself. She seemingly lost her reasoning power. She suffered untold agony. Doctors told her to stay on her medication of Delantin tablets or she would even get worse than she was.

Many times I called her name in prayer. Oh, how I wanted God to heal her! How desperately I wanted God to break the power of evil that tortured her so much! I was waiting on God to do it. But God was waiting for me to do it!

I say this humbly, only to illustrate the Scriptures.

Jesus said, [I give you] *power against unclean spirits, to cast them out, and to heal all manner of sickness and all manner of disease. Go, preach . . . heal the sick, cleanse the lepers, raise the dead, cast out devils: freely ye have received, freely give* (Matthew 10:1,7,8).

Believing God, I went to Dallas, Texas, where my sister lived. When I entered her home, I was greeted by the nurse on duty. I walked into the bedroom, and my sister did not even recognize me. I don't think that I would have recognized her if I had met her on the street. Her eyes were glassy, her face was swollen, and her countenance was different.

I looked at her lying there in that bed of sickness and anger rose up within me. I was mad at the devil and all the power of evil that had caused this. Taking a deep breath, I commanded the devils to depart, and sickness to go, and they did!

Immediately, my sister jumped out of bed and ran through the house, praising God!

Later that day she went to the table and fed herself! Her reasoning came back, and the sickness vanished, never to return! This has been many years ago, and she is still the picture of health.

Later I asked my sister, ''Why did you leap out of bed so suddenly, when I commanded you to?'' She said, ''John, I heard the voice of the Ancient of Days — the Eternal God — say from His throne, 'Rise up and walk.' ''

I said, ''No, Mary, you heard me say that.''

She became adamant in her assertion, ''No, it was not you that I heard, but the voice of God spoke this command to me, 'Rise and walk.' ''

You see, when we step out on the promises of

God, and exercise commanding power, our voice is blended with the voice of Almighty God, and the impossible comes to pass. (You can read my sister's full testimony in my book, *You Can Change Your Destiny*.)

Doing the works of Jesus

As you read the Book of Acts, notice the many times the disciples used this commanding power. They are not found praying for the sick as much as they are found *delivering* the sick.

When Jesus cursed the fig tree and it withered, the disciples were amazed at the power of Jesus' words. But surely, you may say, He doesn't expect us to have such power. Listen to what He says to you:

If ye shall have faith, and doubt not, ye shall not only do this which is done to the fig tree, but also if ye shall say unto this mountain, Be thou removed, and be cast into the sea; ***it shall be done*** (Matthew 21:21, emphasis mine).

Jesus is plainly saying to us that we have the same power to command things to happen, and they will come to pass.

This is not done through a false sense of self-importance. This does not come to pass by "little gods" running around shouting and shaking everything and everybody, because they have become great in their own eyes. When you understand how you heal the sick and drive out diseases, it will give you a sense of humility and utter dependence upon God, who is the Source of all power.

If you were drowning and I cast out a life-saver attached to the rope, and drew you in to safety, what would you say saved you? You might say, "This life-saver saved me," or "This rope did not break, so it saved me." But really, the one who threw it in and pulled you out is the one who really saved you.

So it is with deliverance. Like the life-saver or rope, we are only instruments in deliverance. Behind it all is God in His mighty love and mercy.

If you understand the following secret, it will save you from pride and failure.

Healing the sick

How does a doctor heal? Really a doctor cannot heal, for all healing is from God. He is only an instrument to help. But what does he do to help people? He either takes something out or puts something in. Sometimes both are necessary.

A doctor may take out a bad gallbladder. He may give some internal medicine as a prescription. But you have to cooperate with him. You have to do as he tells you. You have to follow his instructions. No doctor could help you otherwise. If you do not obey his instructions, he cannot help you. He can give the prescription, but if you do not get it filled and take it, all would be to no avail as far as the doctor is concerned.

God tells us to heal the sick. We do it by either taking something out of people, or putting something into people. We must get them to give up and take out the sin which hinders the power of God. We must put into them the message of the cross and the promises of God. It is all connected with the Word of God. We heal them by giving them the Word of God. *He sent his word, and healed them* (Psalm 107:21).

You notice Jesus FIRST says, "Go preach (or teach or give out the Word of God) — then heal the sick, cleanse the leper, cast out devils, etc."

The Bible says Jesus gave the disciples power against unclean spirits, to cast them out, and to heal all manner of sickness and all manner of disease. Where is this power? How do we get it to work? By preaching and teaching — sharing the Gospel! The power is in the Word. The Gospel is the power of God to EVERYONE that believeth!

As we preach the Word of God, we are taking something out and putting something into man. Through the preaching, they repent and give up sin, and receive Jesus and His promises into their hearts. They are freed from Satan, and then we can command them to be free from all the works of Satan.

"Preach the power out!"

If you have the Gospel, you have the power. If you give the Gospel, you give the power. Without the Word, you have no power. "Without Me," says Jesus, "you can do nothing." You don't pray the power down, but preach the power out! A perfect picture of this is found in Acts 14:7-10.

Here a cripple was present in one of the services of Paul the apostle. Paul wanted him healed. Paul knew that he could heal him in God's way. What was God's way? Preaching the Gospel which told of what Jesus did in bearing our sins, sickness, and curse when He died on the cross. The Bible says Paul preached the Gospel and the lame man heard him speak. The Word produced faith. Paul looked at the man and perceived that he had faith. Now the man was ready to be healed. Paul cried with a loud voice, "Stand upright on thy feet!" And the man was healed instantly and stood!

How did Paul heal him? By teaching him what God did through the sacrifice of Jesus and by giving him the promises of God to produce repentance and faith. Then he got him to act on the Word of God. But behind it all as the Source of power was God, our merciful Heavenly Father.

I have seen this happen many times. After I preach the Gospel, understanding comes as to what God has done through Jesus in bearing the people's sins and sicknesses. I command sickness to depart, and because the people have faith in God, it comes to pass. But without the Gospel and the promises of God, my words are like sounding brass and tinkling cymbals.

A woman came to a meeting with a large tumor. She looked very large in the middle of her body. I commanded the tumor to die and dissolve, and it did! She came back several services after that, and her body gradually became smaller. When I went back to that city in a few weeks, she was a very thin person, with no sign of the tumor. She was healed by hearing me preach the Gospel, but God's power in the Word was behind it all. This has happened countless times in my ministry.

In our crusades in the Philippine Islands and India, we have had crowds in a single service estimated at 15,000 people. They were so lost, so sick, and so filled with fear and torment. Jesus told me to heal and cleanse them. How did I do it? By giving them the Word of God! By preaching to them the Good News about Jesus!

By doing this, I was getting them to repent and accept Jesus. I was getting them to act on the promises of God. When faith rose in their hearts, and they welcomed Jesus as their Savior, I then commanded devils, sickness, and diseases to depart. It worked just like in the Bible! Cripples who were carried in, rose and walked. Little children with clubfeet became whole! The blind, deaf, and mute were delivered! Leprous sores which had drained for years, dried up and were replaced with new skin!

God is a faith God. He works through His Word. The Word of God is living and powerful. No Word of God shall be void of power. The Words of God are "life to all that find them, and health to all their flesh."

Go forth as Jesus commanded you. Heal the sick, cast out devils, and cleanse the lepers. He gave this power to *you*! Exercise this power in the Name of Jesus.

Healing and deliverance is through the Word. Give out the Word. The power of God is in the Gospel. Give out the Gospel. When the needy understand the Gospel, and repent, and turn to Jesus, then command all sickness and trouble to leave in Jesus' Name, and it shall be done!

Chapter 5

How You Can Have a Supernatural Ministry

There is no doubt that God wants all of His children to have a supernatural ministry in bringing deliverance to this needy world. He has made this plain again and again. His power and gifts are not for a select few, but for all believers. The Bible says, *These signs shall follow them that believe; In my name shall they cast out devils; they shall speak with new tongues . . . lay hands on the sick, and they shall recover* (Mark 16:17,18). The Lord said, *The manifestation of the Spirit is given to every man.* He said concerning the gifts of the Spirit that He divides *to every man severally as he will* (1 Corinthians 12:7,11).

The Lord has commanded you to go spread the Gospel. He has told you to cast out devils. He has instructed you to lay hands on the sick that they might recover. He wants to use you by His Spirit to reach the lost, bound, and sick around you.

Jesus said, *Verily, verily, I say unto you, He that believeth on me, the works that I do shall he do also; and greater works than these shall he do; because I go unto my Father. And whatsoever ye shall ask in my name, that will I do . . . If ye shall ask any thing in my name, I will do it* (John 14:12-14).

Following Jesus' example

One day the Apostle Peter was with the rest of the disciples in a boat. He saw Jesus coming to them, walking on the water. This frightened the others, but it thrilled Peter. He said in effect, ''Lord, I see You doing something supernatural and it thrills me. I want to do things like that. Let me come walk on the water like You.''

Did this displease Jesus? Did He rebuke Peter and say, ''You ought to be ashamed of yourself. Don't you know I am the Son of the Living God? What makes you think that you can do what I am doing? Stay in the boat!'' Did He say that? No! It pleased Jesus that one of His disciples wanted to do what He was doing supernaturally. He said to Peter, ''Come!'' And Peter walked on the water! Hallelujah!

One day I was sailing through life in my little Baptist boat. I began to study the Bible in my search for deeper things. As I read Matthew, Mark, Luke, and John, I saw the Son of the Living God. He was healing the sick. He was casting out demons. He was setting the captives free. He was bringing men to God through the power of the Holy Spirit. Oh, how it thrilled me! I cried, ''Jesus, I want to do what I see You doing.'' He said, ''Come!''

Thank God, I marched out of my little Baptist boat and walked out to do what Jesus was doing. Others have stayed in the boat where it is safe. They are not in danger of sinking, but they are not out where the miracles are. Oh, for men and women who will risk all

44

for Jesus. Oh, for people who will rise up and walk out, trusting only in the power of Jesus!

Now perhaps you are in the same place. Are you in a little denominationalized boat, sailing safely through life? Have you seen Jesus as He really is and ever shall be? Have you become dissatisfied with "going in religious circles"? Does your heart cry out to be used of God in this awful hour when the coming of the Lord draws nigh? Then hear the sweet voice of Jesus say to you, "Come. Come My child and do what I have called you to do. March out of that boat even though all others refuse to go with you!" Place Jesus and the will of God above and beyond your denomination. Obey God rather than man.

Signs are for believers

How then can you have a supernatural ministry? What are you to do as you come forth in Jesus' Name?

Jesus said, "These signs shall follow them that believe." Believing is linked to signs. Someone says, "I don't believe in signs and wonders." Then they are not for you. They are for *believers*! Others say, "I don't believe in speaking in tongues, prophesying, casting out devils, healing the sick, and the gifts of the Spirit." Then they are not for you. They are for *believers*. These signs will not follow doubters, but they will follow believers.

Let me mention three things that you as a Spirit-filled Christian must believe to enter into a supernatural ministry.

Knowing who you are

First: **You must believe you are the person God**

says you are. You must know who you are in the sight of God, man, and the devil. God knows far more about you than you do yourself.

Let me talk about you. I am not talking about your body, but you. You, as a spirit, live in a body. One day you will leave the body and live forever with the Lord. It is not your body that sees, feels, hears, talks, and acts, but you on the inside of the body. When you move out, then the body cannot see, feel, hear, talk, and act. But you will still be doing these things throughout eternity. You, down on the inside of that body, is the one I am talking about in this message.

The Bible says, *If any man be in Christ, he is a new creature: old things are passed away; behold, all things are become new* (2 Corinthians 5:17).

This is talking about you inside of that body. When you were saved, you became a new creation. Old things passed away and behold all things became new. God's work of grace was on the inside. This is what the Bible calls the new birth, the washing of regeneration, and the new man (see John 3:3, Titus 3:5, Ephesians 4:24).

During the days I struggled with these things for myself, I constantly read and studied the Bible. One day there came, as it were, a man stepping forth from the pages of Scripture. Not a real man, but one I could see in my spirit. He marched forth in power. He sparkled with the supernatural gifts. He was strong and courageous. Devils trembled as they saw him. He laid his hands on the sick and they recovered. He set the captives free. He walked like the son of a King. Royalty was in his every step. He was more than a conqueror. He knew no fear. And as he went forth he

46

delivered mankind, brought fear to every demon, and gladdened the heart of God.

I said in amazement, "Lord, who is this?" The answer came, "This is a New Testament believer! This is one of the new creatures!"

You and I can be like this if we will only realize who we are. The Bible says concerning this new creature the following things:

There is therefore now no condemnation (Romans 8:1).

We are *created in righteousness and true holiness* (Ephesians 4:24).

He became sin for us *that we might be made the righteousness of God* (2 Corinthians 5:21).

We are *partakers of the divine nature* (2 Peter 1:4).

He *washed us from our sins in his own blood* (Revelation 1:5).

We are *accepted in the beloved* (Ephesians 1:6).

We have everlasting life and shall not perish, but have *passed from death unto life* (John 5:24).

Our names are written in the Lamb's *book of life* (Philippians 4:33).

We are more than conquerors (Romans 8:37).

We *can do all things through Christ which* [strengthens us] (Philippians 4:13).

He took our sins, our sicknesses, our curse, and our death and has set us free. And whom the Son sets free is free indeed (see Isaiah 53:5, Matthew 8:17, Galatians 3:13, John 8:36).

Oh, praise be to His holy Name forever! Let everything that hath breath praise the Lord! Think of this: We have His life, His blood, His nature, His promises, His Name, and His power! *He that spared not his own Son, but delivered him up for us all, how shall he not with him also freely give us all things?* (Romans 8:32).

We are not weak worms of the dust! What God has cleansed call not common nor unclean. We are sons of God! We are children of the King! God looks upon us as though we had never sinned. We are restored! What the first Adam lost, the second Adam, Jesus, gained back for us. We are new creatures! We will hold our heads up high. We are not ashamed. We are not afraid. We are sent forth into the world with a commission from on high. We know that greater is He that is within us than he that is in the world.

No more whining!

No more groveling in the dust!

No more condemning ourselves!

Inside of our body of clay stands a new person who has been fashioned by the mighty hands of God.

Knowing where you are

Second, **You must believe you are where God says you are.** You must recognize your present sphere of life and activity. What does God say about it? He says, [He] *hath delivered us from the power of darkness, and hath translated us into the kingdom of his dear Son* (Colossians 1:13).

There are two kingdoms in this world. The kingdom of darkness and the Kingdom of His dear Son. Once you were in the kingdom of darkness. There, Satan had power over you. The Bible says he is the *spirit that now worketh in the children of disobedience* and, he takes people *captive at his will*

(Ephesians 2:2, 2 Timothy 2:26).

But when God saved you and you became a new creature, He translated you out of the power and authority of darkness and into the Kingdom of God. Notice the past tense — hath — hath — hath. It is not something that *will* happen, but it is *already* a reality. You once stood in darkness under the power of Satan and looked out at the Kingdom of God where people served Jesus with joy in their hearts. Now you stand with Jesus looking out into the kingdom of darkness where multitudes still live in need of salvation.

You have been translated out to help others get out. You have been delivered to help get others delivered. You have been released to release others. You are free from the power of Satan that you might go forth and free others. You were saved by the help, prayers, witnessing, and action of other Christians. You must do the same for others.

Satan has no power or authority over you as a new creature. Satan fears and trembles in your presence. The Bible says, *Resist the devil and he will flee* [run in terror] *from you* (James 4:7).

Because you are now out of Satan's kingdom and in the Kingdom of God, Jesus says to you, *I give you power and authority over all devils* (Luke 9:1), and *Behold, I give unto you power to tread on serpents and scorpions, and over all the power of the enemy: and nothing shall by any means hurt you* (Luke 10:19).

Jesus said in effect, "Don't ask Me to do it because I've given this power to you! *You* cast out devils! *You* deliver the captives! *You* tread on serpents and scorpions! In My Name, you can do these things!

"Lift up your head, new creature! You are in the

Kingdom of His dear Son and the devil has no power over you! You have been given all power over him in My Name!''

Believe you can do what God says you can do

Let us go one step further. The third thing you must do to launch forth successfully is this: **You must believe you can do the things God says you can do, and believe it so strongly you actually start doing them.**

Here is where so many fail.

For a long time I stayed in my office praying for the gifts of the Spirit to operate in my life after I received the baptism in the Holy Spirit. Nothing happened. I don't know what I expected. I suppose I thought an angel would come down like a little fairy and hit me on the head with a wand and announce to me that certain gifts would now come forth in my life.

God seemed to say to me one day, ''What good would a spiritual gift do you now in your office if I gave it to you? There are no sick here to be healed. There are no captives here to be delivered. There are no lost here to be won. Go forth and stand before the needy peoples of the world and preach My Word and I will be present to confirm MY WORD.''

I decided I could do what God said I could do no matter how I felt. I knew God could not lie. He said I could do these things so I launched forth. I arranged a citywide meeting not far from my home town. Hundreds came. I stood there on the platform and told them why Jesus died and rose again. I told them what He said I could do. He said I could cast out devils, lay hands on the sick and they would recover, and set the captives free. I invited them to test the Lord by coming for help. To my utter amazement it looked like EVERYONE came. Such a line of people! What a challenge!

The devil said, "What are you going to do when they don't get delivered?" I said, "Devil, what are you going to do when they *do* get delivered?"

The first man to come was a Spanish man about 30 years old. He had a mute spirit and could not talk. A hush came over the audience. I did what Jesus said I could do. I acted like He told me the truth. I commanded that dumb spirit to leave the man. The spirit obeyed my voice as I spoke in the Name of Jesus. I placed the microphone up to the man's mouth and asked him to say something. He said, "Thank You, Jesus!" The crowd began to shout and praise the Lord! The move was on and it has been on ever since for me.

Since that time I have gone all over the nation, Canada, Mexico, Central America, South America, India, Europe, the Philippine Islands, and many other parts of the world doing the same thing. I expect to meet at least a million souls one of these days around the throne of God who have been redeemed out of these countries. Hallelujah!

I challenge you to do these three things:

• Believe that you are the person God says you are.

• Believe you are where God says you are.

• Believe you can do what God says you can do and begin to act like it today.

You will discover that Jesus is present as you preach His Word. He will confirm His promises. He will perform whatever you ask in His Name. You will rejoice, knowing that God watches over His Word to perform it.

Rise up new creature! Stand tall for Jesus! Look around you! You are in the Kingdom of His dear Son! Assault the kingdom of Satan in Jesus' Name. Millions wait for the message of grace and mercy. Millions await the sound of your footsteps coming to their rescue with the Gospel.

Now you know! You will never be the same! Nothing can stop you! Time is flying and men are dying! The King's business requireth haste!

BOOKS BY JOHN OSTEEN

A Miracle for Your Marriage
Believing God for Your Loved Ones
Healed of Cancer by Dodie Osteen
How To Claim the Benefits of the Will
How To Demonstrate Satan's Defeat
How To Flow in the Super Supernatural
How To Release the Power of God
Overcoming Hindrances to Receiving the Baptism in the
   Holy Spirit
Pulling Down Strongholds
Reigning in Life as a King
Rivers of Living Water
Six Lies the Devil Uses to Destroy Marriages by Lisa Osteen
The Believer's #1 Need
The Bible Way to Spiritual Power
The Confessions of a Baptist Preacher
The Divine Flow
The 6th Sense . . . Faith
The Truth Shall Set You Free
There Is a Miracle in Your Mouth
This Awakening Generation
Unraveling the Mystery of the Blood Covenant
What To Do When the Tempter Comes
You Can Change Your Destiny

MINIBOOKS

A Place Called There
ABC's of Faith
Deception! Recognizing True and False Ministries
Four Principles in Receiving From God
How To Minister Healing to the Sick
How To Receive Life Eternal
Keep What God Gives
Love & Marriage
Receive the Holy Spirit
Saturday's Coming
What To Do When Nothing Seems to Work
Selected titles also available in Spanish

Please write for a complete list of prices in the John Osteen Faith
Library Catalog. MANNA magazine is also available upon
request, free and postage paid.

John Osteen Ministries
P.O. Box 23117
Houston, Texas 77228